Introduction

Are you looking for flavorful recipes that make eating healthy easier?

Do you want mouth-watering dishes without compromising your cholesterol levels?

Are you ready to take the next step towards a balanced diet?

We all want to be healthy and feel our best, but it's not always easy to find the right mix of flavorful recipes and the cholesterol-lowering ingredients we need. The good news is that with this cookbook, you can have the best of both worlds – delicious, flavorful recipes and powerful, cholesterol-lowering ingredients.

Here's what you'll find inside:

- **Lose Weight & Keep Cholesterol Levels Balanced:** Learn how to fill your plate with the right types of food that help you lose weight and lower bad cholesterol.
- **Quick & Healthy Recipes:** Cook up tasty dishes with minimal effort - you don't have to sacrifice flavor for health!
- **Power Ingredients:** Get the biggest nutritional bang for your buck with cholesterol-lowering power foods like spinach, nuts, dark chocolate, and red wine.
- **Mouthwatering Photos:** Get inspired with pictures of each delectable dish and make meal planning easy.

Take charge of your health and let this cookbook help you create flavorful meals with ingredients that make a

Low Cholesterol Cooking Made Easy

Recipes to Enjoy Meals without Compromising on Flavor

Contents

difference. Get your copy of this cookbook today and start feeling your best.

Appetizers

Recipe 1. Spiced Nuts

Cooking Time: 10 minutes

Servings: 4 cups

The List of Ingredients:

1. 1 cup halve pecans
2. 2 egg whites
3. ¾ cup Splenda sugar substitute
4. 2 tsp. cayenne pepper
5. 1 cup halved filbert nuts

6. 3 tsp. cinnamon

7. 1 cup halved walnuts

8. 1 cup halved peanuts

Method:

Step 1   Whip the egg white with 4 tbsp. of water.

Step 2   Coat the nuts with the egg white mixture.

Step 3   Drain any excess egg white.

Step 4   Combine the Splenda, cinnamon and cayenne pepper in a bowl or bag.

Step 5   Transfer the nuts to the spice mix and thoroughly coat.

Step 6   Place a single layer of nuts on a baking sheet and bake at 350 for 5 minutes.

Step 7   Stir the nuts and cook for another 4-5 minutes.

Recipe 2. Hummus

Cooking Time: 0

Servings: 3 cups

The List of Ingredients:

1. ¼ cup lemon juice
2. Salt to taste
3. 30 oz. of canned chickpeas with liquid
4. 3 tsp. curry
5. 3 tbsp. sesame tahini

6. 3 garlic cloves

7. Dash of hot sauce - optional

Method:

Step 1   Combine the garlic, curry, tahini, lemon juice and salt in a bowl.

Step 2   Transfer the chickpeas and their liquid to a food processor and start to pulse.

Step 3   Slowly add the dressing until you have a smooth, creamy consistency.

Step 4   Refrigerate until you serve.

Recipe 3. Guacamole

Cooking Time: 0

Servings: 1 ½ cup

The List of Ingredients:

1. 1/3 cup diced tomatoes
2. 2 tbsp. chopped cilantro
3. Salt to taste
4. 2 tbsp. lime juice
5. 2 tbsp. chopped onion

6. 1 tsp. minced garlic

7. 2 avocados

Method:

Step 1   Cut the avocados open and spoon out the flesh.

Step 2   Put the avocado flesh in a bowl and mash.

Step 3   Stir in the remaining ingredients and refrigerate for 2 hours.

Recipe 4. Honey Roasted Cashews

Cooking Time: 12 minutes

Servings: 2 cups

The List of Ingredients:

1. 2 cups whole cashews
2. 1 tsp. cinnamon
3. ½ tsp. salt
4. 4 tbsp. honey
5. 1 tbsp. coconut nut oil

6. ¼ cup Splenda sweetener

Method:

Step 1   Placed the cashews on a baking sheet.

Step 2   Bake at 325 degrees for 12 minutes. Stir the cashews a few times.

Step 3   Combine the sweetener, cinnamon and salt in a bowl and set aside.

Step 4   Combine the honey and coconut oil with 3 tbsp. of water in another bowl.

Step 5   Pour the mixture in a small pan and coat the cashews. Let sit for 5 minutes.

Step 6   Stir the cashews into the sweetener mixture.

Step 7   Line a baking sheet with waxed paper and transfer the cashews to the baking sheet.

Step 8   Let cool.

Recipe 5. Ranch Dip

Cooking Time: 0

Servings: 1 ½ cups

The List of Ingredients:

1. ½ cup low-fat sour cream
2. 1 tsp. basil
3. Dash of cayenne pepper
4. 1 tsp. horseradish
5. 3 tbsp. chopped onions

6. ¼ tsp. Mrs. Dash seasoning

7. 1 cup non-fat Greek yogurt

Method:

Step 1   Blend all ingredients thoroughly and refrigerate for 6 hours.

Breakfast

Recipe 6. Cottage Cheese Danish

Cooking Time: 13 minutes

Servings: 2

The List of Ingredients:

1. 2 slices of bread, whole wheat or any other kind
2. 2 tsp. cinnamon
3. 1 tsp. almond extract
4. 1 cup low-fat cottage cheese
5. 2 tsp. Stevia sweetener

Method:

Step 1   Place the bread in oven and toast for 5 mins at 350 degrees.

Step 2   While the bread is toasting, combine the cottage cheese, sweetener, cinnamon and almond extract in a bowl.

Step 3   Remove the bread from oven and top the side that has been toasted with the cream cheese mixture.

Step 4   Return the bread mixture to the oven for 8 minutes, until the bottom side toasts and the cottage cheese starts to bubble.

Step 5   Enjoy while the Danish is hot.

Recipe 7. Spinach Omelet

Cooking Time: 10 minutes

Servings: 2

The List of Ingredients:

1. Dash of garlic powder
2. Dash of salt and pepper
3. 4 large eggs
4. 3 tbsp. chopped onion
5. 1 tsp canola oil

6. 2 tbsp. chopped parsley

7. ½ cup baby spinach

Method:

Step 1   Add the salt, pepper and garlic powder to the beaten egg.

Step 2   Heat the oil in a skillet.

Step 3   Sauté the onions for 5 minutes, then add the spinach and parsley and cook for 2 more minutes.

Step 4   Pour the eggs on the spinach mixture.

Step 5   Slide the eggs mixture in the skillet until the edges begin to set.

Step 6   Cook for 3 minutes, until the omelet is almost set.

Step 7   Use a spatula to fold half of the omelet over the other.

Step 8   Cook another minute and lift the omelet to a plate.

Step 9   Adjust the salt and pepper to your taste or use Mrs. Dash seasoning.

Step 10   Cut the omelet in half, one half per serving.

Recipe 8. Granola Nut Bars

Cooking Time: 40 minutes

Servings: 6

The List of Ingredients:

1. 1 1/2 cups unsweetened applesauce
2. 1 tsp cinnamon
3. 1 cup rolled oats
4. ¼ carob chips
5. 3 egg whites

6. ¼ cup chopped walnuts

7. ¼ cup raisins

Method:

Step 1	Stir the egg white, applesauce and cinnamon together in a bowl.
Step 2	Gently add the remaining ingredients.
Step 3	Transfer to a square baking dish lined with parchment paper.
Step 4	Fold in oats, raisins, walnut and carob chips.
Step 5	Bake for 40 minutes at 350 degrees.
Step 6	Let the granola cool before cutting into bars.

Recipe 9. Whole Wheat Banana Muffins

Cooking Time: 20 minutes

Servings: 12

The List of Ingredients:

1. ¼ cup unsweetened applesauce
2. 2 beaten eggs
3. 1 tsp. baking soda
4. ½ tsp. nutmeg

5. 4 mashed bananas

6. 3 tbsp. wheat germ

7. 1 cup whole wheat flour

8. 1 tsp. cinnamon

9. 1 cup oat flour

10. ½ cup plain low-fat yogurt

11. 1 tbsp. vanilla extract

Method:

Step 1   Preheat the oven to 375 degrees.

Step 2   Fill a 12-cup muffin pan with the paper liners.

Step 3   Stir together the eggs, yogurt, applesauce, mashed bananas and vanilla.

Step 4   In another bowl, combine the whole wheat flour, oat flour, wheat germ, baking soda, cinnamon and nutmeg.

Step 5   Add the flour to the banana mixture and combine well.

Step 6   Distribute the batter onto the muffin pan.

Step 7   Bake for 20 minutes.

Recipe 10. Oatmeal Pancakes

Cooking Time: 27 minutes

Servings: 3

The List of Ingredients:

1. 3 egg whites
2. Dash of salt
3. ½ cup quick-cooking oatmeal
4. 3 tbsp. honey
5. 1 tsp. cinnamon

6. 4 tbsp. no-fat milk

Method:

Step 1   Combine all ingredients in a bowl.

Step 2   Coat a skillet with non-stick spray.

Step 3   Pour 1/3 of the batter into the skillet and cook for 5 minutes.

Step 4   Flip the pancake and cook for another 4 minutes.

Step 5   Repeat twice with the remaining batter.

Step 6   Top the pancakes with strawberries or sugar-free syrup.

Recipe 11. Avocado Toast

Cooking Time: 5 minutes

Servings: 1

The List of Ingredients:

1. 2 slices whole wheat bread
2. 1/8 tsp. toasted sesame seeds
3. Dash of lemon juice
4. 2 tbsp. chopped parsley
5. Dash of salt

6. ½ avocado

Method:

Step 1   Toast the whole wheat bread, about 5 minutes.

Step 2   Mash the avocado and stir in the remaining ingredients.

Step 3   Spoon the avocado on top of the toast.

Main Meals

Chicken

Recipe 12. Sweet and Sour Chicken

Cooking Time: 35 minutes

Servings: 4

The List of Ingredients:

1. ½ lb. shredded chicken thighs
2. 1 chopped green bell pepper
3. 2 tbsp. olive oil
4. 2 cups prepared white or brown rice
5. 4 tbsp. honey

6. 1 chopped onion
7. 4 oz. diced pineapple with juice
8. 4 tbsp. Truvia brown sugar substitute
9. 1 cup sugar-free tomato sauce
10. 1 ½ cups low-sodium chicken broth
11. ¼ tsp. Mrs. Dash seasoning
12. 2 tbsp. white wine vinegar

Method:

Step 1   Prepare the rice according to Method:

Step 2   Heat the oil in a skillet and sauté the onion and bell pepper for 5 minutes.

Step 3   Stir in the remaining ingredients except the chicken and the rice.

Step 4   Simmer the sauce for 15 minutes.

Step 5   Add the chicken and simmer for another 15 minutes, until the chicken is cooked.

Step 6   Serve the chicken and sauce over rice.

Recipe 13. Turkey and Avocado Sandwich

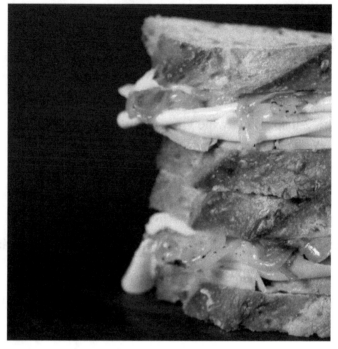

Cooking Time: 0

Servings: 2

The List of Ingredients:

1. 2 slices Swiss cheese
2. 4 slices turkey bacon
3. 4 slices whole wheat bread – toasting is optional
4. 1 sliced avocado

5. 2 tbsp. low-fat mayonnaise

6. 4 oz. sliced turkey breast

7. 1 sliced tomato

Method:

Step 1   If using mayonnaise, spread on two slices of bread.

Step 2   Top the slices with turkey, turkey bacon, cheese, avocado slices and tomato slices.

Step 3   Cover with the remaining 2 slices to create sandwiches.

Step 4   Don't forget the pickles!

Recipe 14. Greek-Style Chicken and Pasta

Cooking Time: 16 minutes

Servings: 4

The List of Ingredients:

1. 4 tbsp. chopped parsley

2. 4 tbsp. sliced Kalamata olives

3. ½ cup red wine

4. ½ cup fat-free half and half

5. 1 small chopped onion

6. ¾ cup crumbled feta cheese

7. 1 tsp. Mrs. Dash seasoning

8. 1 tbsp. olive oil

9. 1 lb. cubed or shredded chicken meat

10. 2 cups pasta of choice

11. ¼ cup grated parmesan cheese

12. 3 tbsp. capers

13. 2 tbsp. lemon juice

14. 1 cup diced tomatoes

15. 1 ½ cup chopped marinated artichoke hearts

16. 2 minced garlic cloves

Method:

Step 1   Cook the pasta according to directions and drain. Set aside.

Step 2   Heat the olive oil in a skillet and sauté the onion and garlic for 3 minutes.

Step 3   Add the chicken and cook for about 5 minutes, until the chicken is no longer pink.

Step 4   Reduce the heat to a simmer and add the remaining ingredients, except the olives, parmesan cheese and capers.

Step 5   Stir well and simmer for 8 minutes.

Step 6   Top with olives, parmesan cheese and capers
           when serving.

Recipe 15. Chicken Lo Mein

Cooking Time: 16 minutes

Servings: 4

The List of Ingredients:

1. 1 tbsp. grated ginger
2. ½ cup shredded carrots
3. 1 ½ cups diced bell peppers
4. ½ cup water chestnuts
5. 2 minced garlic cloves

6. 2 cups snow peas

7. 4 tbsp. low sodium soy sauce

8. 2 tbsp. oyster sauce

9. 8 ounces angel hair pasta

10. ¾ cup low sodium chicken broth

11. 1 diced onion

12. 2 tbsp. cornstarch

13. ½ cup baby corn

14. 2 tbsp. sesame seed oil

15. 1 cup cooked shredded chicken

16. 1 ½ cups sliced mushrooms

Method:

Step 1   Prepare the pasta according to direction, then drain and set aside.

Step 2   Combine the broth, soy sauce, oyster sauce and cornstarch in a bowl.

Step 3   Heat the sesame seed oil in a large skillet and sauté the garlic and ginger for 2 minutes.

Step 4   Add the mushrooms, bell peppers, and onion and stir for 4 minutes.

Step 5   Pour the broth mix into the skillet and add the snow peas, grated carrots, baby corn, water chestnuts and shredded chicken. Stir well.

Step 6   Simmer for 10 minutes.

Step 7   Transfer the cooked pasta and vegetables to a bowl and toss to combine.

Recipe 16. Chicken Stew

Cooking Time: 40 minutes

Servings: 4

The List of Ingredients:

1. 2 cubed chicken breasts or thighs
2. 1 ¼ cup low-sodium chicken broth
3. 2 cups cubed sweet potatoes
4. ¼ tsp. grated ginger
5. 1 cup fresh spinach

6. 2 cloves garlic, minced

7. Salt and pepper to taste

8. 1/8 tsp. chipotle powder

9. 1 small chopped onion

10. 2 tbsp. olive oil

Method:

Step 1   Heat the olive oil in a pan or skillet

Step 2   Sauté onion for about 5 minutes, then add in the garlic and cook for another 2 minutes.

Step 3   Stir in remaining ingredients except spinach and stir.

Step 4   Bring the broth to boil.

Step 5   Reduce the heat to a simmer and cook for 30 minutes.

Step 6   Add the spinach, stir, and cook for 3 minutes until spinach is wilted.

Recipe 17. Chicken Pasta with Asparagus

Cooking Time: 22 minutes

Servings: 4

The List of Ingredients:

1. 1/3 cup grated Parmesan cheese
2. ½ tsp. poultry seasoning
3. 2 tbsp. red pepper flakes
4. 2 tbsp. olive oil

5. 2 cups cooked whole wheat pasta

6. 2 minced garlic gloves

7. 4 cubed chicken breasts

8. 1 cup chopped red peppers

9. 1 cup of trimmed and chopped asparagus spears

10. 1 cup sliced mushrooms

11. ¼ cup white wine

12. 1 small diced onion

13. ½ cup low-sodium chicken broth

Directions

Step 1   Cook the pasta according to directions. Set aside.

Step 2   Heat the olive oil in a large skillet.

Step 3   Season the chicken with poultry seasoning, salt and pepper.

Step 4   Sauté the chicken for 5 minutes.

Step 5   Add the onion and garlic and cook for another 3 minutes.

Step 6   Transfer the chicken to a platter.

Step 7   Add all remaining ingredients except the cheese to the skillet and stir well.

Step 8   Cook for 10 minutes, until the vegetables are done.

Step 9   Stir in the Parmesan cheese and let it melt for 2 minutes.

Step 10   Return and chicken and pasta to the skillet and then cook for 2 minutes.

Recipe 18. Chicken Creole

Cooking Time: 6 hours

Servings: 4

The List of Ingredients:

1. 3 diced celery stalks
2. ¾ cup white wine
3. 1 tsp. Worcestershire sauce
4. 4 skinless chicken breasts cut into bite-sized pieces
5. 1 diced onion

6. 3 cups crushed tomatoes with liquid

7. 4 cup diced bell pepper

8. ¼ tsp. or more Creole seasoning

9. 4 minced garlic gloves

10. 1 or 2 tsp. hot sauce

11. ¼ tsp. Mrs. Dash seasoning

Method:

Step 1   Season the chicken with Mrs. Dash

Step 2   Place the chicken and remaining ingredients in the slow cooker and stir well.

Step 3   Cook on high for 6 hours.

Beef

Recipe 19. Shepherd's Pie

Cooking Time: 48 minutes

Servings: 4

The List of Ingredients:

1. 1 tsp. olive oil
2. Salt and pepper to taste
3. 1 small diced onion
4. ½ tsp. sage
5. 1 lb. ground beef

6. 1 ½ cup frozen peas and carrots
7. ½ cup low-fat shredded cheddar cheese
8. 1 cup low-sodium beef broth
9. 1 cup mashed potatoes (see recipes)

Method:

Step 1   Preheat oven to 350 degrees

Step 2   Use non-stick spray to coat a casserole dish.

Step 3   Heat the oil in a skillet and sauté the onions for 5 minutes.

Step 4   Brown the beef for 8 minutes.

Step 5   Add the beef broth and frozen peas and carrots.

Step 6   Stir the ingredients and cook for 5 minutes, until any liquid has evaporated.

Step 7   Transfer the meat and vegetables to the casserole dish.

Step 8   Top with the prepared potatoes.

Step 9   Sprinkle the cheese on top

Step 10   Bake for 30 minutes.

Recipe 20. Broccoli Beef

Cooking Time: 20 minutes

Servings: 4

Ingredients

1. 3 cups broccoli florets
2. 2 tbsp. grated ginger
3. 2 tbsp. low sodium soy sauce
4. 1 ¼ cup low-sodium beef broth
5. 1 diced onion

6. 1 tbsp. sugar

7. 2 tbsp. minced garlic

8. 1 sliced green pepper

9. 4 tbsp. cornstarch

10. 1 tbsp. olive oil

Method:

Step 1   Combine the cornstarch, soy sauce, and sugar and set aside.

Step 2   Next heat the olive oil in a skillet.

Step 3   Sauté the onion and green pepper for 5 minutes.

Step 4   Stir in the ginger and garlic and cook for another 3 minutes.

Step 5   Add the beef slices and cook for 2 minutes.

Step 6   Pour the beef broth and cornstarch into the skillet, add the broccoli and stir well.

Step 7   Simmer for 10 minutes.

Recipe 21. Bolognese Sauce

Cooking Time: 3 hours 40 minutes

Servings: 6

The List of Ingredients:

1. 32 oz. can diced tomatoes
2. ½ cup low-sodium beef broth
3. 4 minced garlic cloves
4. Salt and pepper to taste
5. 1 lb. cooked pasta

6. 1 cut bell pepper
7. 1 cup soy milk
8. 2 diced onions
9. 1 cup white wine
10. ½ tsp. oregano
11. 2 lb. ground turkey
12. ¾ tbsp. tomato paste
13. ½ cup grated low-fat parmesan cheese

1 tsp. basil

Method:

Step 1   Brown the meat, onion, garlic, zucchini, bell pepper, herbs, salt and pepper in a large pot for 10 minutes.

Step 2   Add the milk and simmer for 15 minutes.

Step 3   Stir in the broth and wine and simmer for another 15 minutes.

Step 4   Add the tomatoes and tomato paste and simmer the sauce for 3 hours.

Step 5   Top with pasta with the Bolognese sauce.

Step 6   Sprinkle with parmesan cheese.

Recipe 22. Stuffed Peppers

Cooking Time: 1 hour 8 minutes

Servings: 6

The List of Ingredients:

1. 2 tsp. Worcestershire sauce
2. 1 tsp. sugar
3. Salt and pepper to taste
4. 1 tbsp. olive oil
5. ¼ tsp. cumin

6. 1 chopped onion

7. 1 chopped jalapeno pepper

8. ½ cup brown rice

9. ½ tsp. oregano

10. 1 lb. ground turkey meat

11. 2 cups low sodium tomato sauce

12. 2 minced garlic cloves

13. 6 bell peppers

Method:

Step 1   Cook the brown rice according to directions.

Step 2   Preheat the oven to 350 degrees.

Step 3   Heat the olive oil in a skillet.

Step 4   Brown the turkey meat for 3 minutes.

Step 5   Stir in the chopped jalapeno, onion, garlic, herbs, salt and pepper.

Step 6   Cook for another 5 minutes.

Step 7   Drain any fat from the skillet.

Step 8   Cut the tops off the bell pepper and remove the seeds and membranes.

Step 9   Place the peppers on a baking sheet.

Step 10   In a large bowl, combine the beef, cooked rice, Worcestershire sauce and 1 cup tomato sauce.

Step 11   Adjust the seasoning, if necessary.

Step 12   Spoon the filling into the peppers.

Step 13   Pour the remaining tomato sauce over the peppers.

Step 14   Bake for 1 hour.

Pork

Recipe 23. Pork Chops with Caramelized Apples

Cooking Time: 28 minutes

Servings: 4

The List of Ingredients:

1. 1 tbsp. cornstarch

2. ½ cup white wine

3. Dash of nutmeg

4. 1 tbsp. unsalted butter

5. 2 sliced Granny Smith apples

6. 1 sliced onion

7. Dash of cinnamon

8. 3 tsp. chopped walnuts

9. Salt and pepper to taste

10. 2 tsp. Truvia – brown sugar substitute

11. ½ tsp. garlic powder

12. ½ cup apple cider

13. 1 tbsp. olive oil

14. ½ cup low-sodium soy sauce

15. 4 pork chops

Method:

Step 1   Combine the soy sauce and white wine in a bowl.

Step 2   Season the pork chop with garlic powder and add to the marinade.

Step 3   Refrigerate overnight.

Step 4   Heat 1 tsp. olive oil in a skillet and brown the chops for 8 minutes, until they are done.

Step 5   Combine the Truvia, cinnamon, nutmeg, salt and pepper.

Step 6   While the chops are browning, add 1 tbsp. butter to a second skillet and sauté the onion for 5 minutes.

Step 7   Add the seasoning mix and apples slices and stir

Step 8   Stir the apple cider and cornstarch together.

Step 9   Pour the cider over the apple slices until the apples are tender, about 15 minutes.

Step 10   Transfer the pork chops to a platter and top with the apple mixture.

Recipe 24. Cuban-Style Pork

Cooking Time: 6 hours 13 minutes

Servings: 6

The List of Ingredients:

1. 2-lb. pork butt
2. 4 sliced garlic cloves
3. 1 tbsp. olive oil
4. 1 tsp. marjoram
5. 2 tbsp. lime juice

6. 1/8 tsp. pepper

7. 1 cup wine

8. 2 tsp. garlic powder

9. 3 cups chicken broth

10. 1 chopped onion

Method:

Step 1   Place all ingredients, except the olive oil, onion and garlic in a slow cooker and stir thoroughly.

Step 2   Cook on high for 6 hours.

Step 3   Transfer the pork to a platter and shred the meat with a fork.

Step 4   Heat olive oil in a skillet and fry the pork for 5 minutes.

Step 5   Stir in onion and garlic then cook for 8 minutes.

Step 6   Enjoy with rice and beans.

Step 7   Serve with lime slices

Recipe 25. Pork Chops with Creamy Sauce

Cooking Time:

Servings: 4

The List of Ingredients:

1. 1 tbsp. butter
2. ¼ tsp. lemon pepper
3. 4 tbsp. white flour
4. 4 tbsp. fat-free sour cream

5. ¼ tsp. garlic salt

6. 2 minced garlic cloves

7. 1 tbsp. Worcestershire sauce

8. 4 chops

9. 1 tsp. lemon juice

10. 1/4 cup soy milk

11. 1 tbsp. agave nectar

Method:

Step 1   Season the pork chops with lemon pepper and garlic salt.

Step 2   Place the flour in a shallow bowl and dredge the chops, shaking off the excess.

Step 3   Heat the butter in a skillet and brown the pork chop and garlic for 3 minutes each side.

Step 4   Combine the sour cream, soy milk, lemon juice, agave nectar and Worcestershire sauce in a bowl.

Step 5   Spoon the sauce over the pork and simmer for 25-30 minutes

Recipe 26. Pork Tenderloin in Wine Sauce

Cooking Time: 50 minutes

Servings: 6

The List of Ingredients:

1. 1 packet brown gravy mix
2. ½ tsp. sliced garlic
3. Salt and pepper to taste
4. 1 cup low-sodium beef broth

5. 2 lb. pork tenderloin
6. 1 tbsp. olive oil

Method:

Step 1   Preheat the oven to 350 degrees.

Step 2   Heat the olive oil in a skillet and brown the pork for 5 minutes each side.

Step 3   Place the pork on a flat surface and cut small nicks into the pork loin and fill them with the garlic slices.

Step 4   Season with salt and pepper

Step 5   Transfer the pork loin to a baking dish and stir in the red wine, broth and gravy mix.

Step 6   Roast for 45 minutes.

Step 7   Slice the pork loin and serve with gravy and healthy mashed potatoes (see recipe)

Soups

Recipe 27. Jambalaya

Cooking Time: 1 hour

Servings: 8

The List of Ingredients:

1. 2 chopped onions
2. 1 lb. peeled and deveined shrimp
3. 1 diced chili pepper
4. 3 cups low-sodium chicken broth
5. 1 ½ cup white or brown rice

6. Hot sauce to taste

7. 1 tbsp. olive oil

8. 2 tbsp. minced garlic

9. Salt and pepper to taste

10. 1 tbsp. Cajun seasoning

11. 2 diced celery stalks

12. 1 chopped bell pepper

13. 30 oz. diced tomatoes with juices

14. 1 lb. ground turkey or chicken sausage meat or sliced chorizo sausage

Method:

Step 1	Heat the oil in a Dutch oven.
Step 2	Sauté the onion for 5 minutes.
Step 3	Stir in the garlic and cook for 3 more minutes.
Step 4	Add all ingredients except the rice and shrimp and stir well.
Step 5	Bring the liquid to a boil, then simmer for 45 minutes.
Step 6	While the jambalaya is cooking, prepare the rice according to directions.
Step 7	Add the shrimp to the jambalaya and cook for 5 more minutes.
Step 8	Serve over rice.

Recipe 28. Potato and Ham Soup

Cooking Time: 40 minutes

Servings: 4

The List of Ingredients:

1. 1 cup cubed ham
2. 3 ½ cups low-sodium chicken broth
3. 1/2 cup chopped celery
4. 4 chopped carrots
5. 1 large diced onion

6. 4 quartered potatoes

7. Dash of Mrs. Dash

Method:

Step 1   Place all ingredients in a large pot.

Step 2   Bring the liquid to boil, then simmer for 30 minutes.

Step 3   Use a slotted spoon to remove the potatoes and mash them with a potato masher.

Step 4   Stir the mashed potatoes back into the pot. This will thicken the broth.

Step 5   Cook for 8 minutes.

Recipe 29. Cabbage Soup

Cooking Time: 1 hours

Servings: 6

The List of Ingredients:

1. 3 cups tomato juice, or more if needed
2. 4 chopped carrots
3. ½ tsp. cumin
4. 2 chopped onions
5. 2 cups chopped zucchini

6. 1 tsp. Worcestershire sauce

7. 1 cup chopped celery

8. 1 packet onion soup mix

9. 1 chopped green pepper

10. ½ lb. ground turkey meat.

11. 2 cups diced tomatoes and liquid

12. ½ tsp. chili powder

13. 2 cups low-sodium beef broth

14. ½ tsp. Mrs. Dash seasoning

15. 2 cups chopped cabbage

Method:

Step 1   Brown the ground turkey meat in a skillet on low heat for 5 minutes.

Step 2   Place the turkey and all other ingredients in a pot and stir well.

Step 3   Make sure the vegetables are covered with liquid.

Step 4   Bring the liquid to a boil.

Step 5   Lower the heat to a simmer and cook for 1 hour, or until the vegetables are done.

Recipe 30. Lentil Soup

Cooking Time: 1 hour 7 minutes

Servings:

The List of Ingredients: 6

1. 2 sliced carrots
2. 4 cubed potatoes
3. 2 minced garlic cloves
4. 1 ham bone
5. 1 tbsp. tomato paste

6. 2 small chopped onions

7. 4 tbsp. cider vinegar

8. 1 tsp. sugar or more to taste

9. 1 cup brown lentils

10. 5 cups low-sodium vegetable broth

11. ½ tsp. oregano

12. 2 bay leaves

13. Salt and pepper to taste

Directions

Step 1   Heat the olive oil in a Dutch oven and then sauté the onion for 5 minutes.

Step 2   Add garlic. Cook for another 2 minutes.

Step 3   Stir in remaining ingredients and then bring the liquid to boil.

Step 4   Reduce heat and simmer for 1 hour.

Step 5   Remove the ham bone and bay leaves and adjust the seasoning.

Seafood

Recipe 31. Shrimp Alfredo

Cooking Time: 33 minutes

Servings: 2

The List of Ingredients:

1. 3 tbsp. white or gluten-free flour
2. ½ cup chicken broth
3. 2 cups prepared regular or whole wheat fettuccine pasta
4. 3 minced garlic cloves

5. ½ cup of grated fat-free Parmesan cheese
6. Salt and pepper to taste
7. 1 cup skim evaporated milk
8. ½ lb. shelled and deveined small or medium shrimp
9. 1 cup fat-free milk
10. 1 tbsp. olive oil

Method:

Step 1   Heat the olive oil in a large skillet and sauté the garlic for 3 minutes.

Step 2   Add the skim milk, evaporated milk, broth, flour, salt and pepper and stir well.

Step 3   Simmer for about 20 minutes or until the sauce thickens and keep stirring frequently.

Step 4   Add the shrimp to the sauce.

Step 5   Cook for another 10 minutes until the shrimp is no longer pink and stir in the grated cheese.

Step 6   Place the cooked pasta in a bowl and toss with the shrimp alfredo sauce.

Recipe 32. Cod with Crumb Topping

Cooking Time: 12 minutes

Servings: 4

The List of Ingredients:

1. 1 tsp. olive oil
2. 3 tbsp. shredded cheddar cheese
3. 2 tbsp. non-fat mayonnaise
4. ½ tsp. Old Bay Seasoning
5. Dash of garlic salt

6. Dash of pepper
7. 1 tbsp. lemon juice
8. 4 cod fillets
9. 1/3 cup bread crumbs

Method:

Step 1	Preheat the oven to 450 degrees.
Step 2	Season the cod fillets with Old Bay Seasoning, pepper and garlic salt.
Step 3	Combine the breadcrumbs, cheddar cheese, olive oil in a bowl.
Step 4	Stir together the non-fat mayonnaise and lemon juice in another bowl.
Step 5	Place the cod fillets in a baking dish.
Step 6	Brush the fish with the mayonnaise mixture, then top with the breadcrumb mixture.
Step 7	Bake for 12 minutes. The cod should be flaky.

Recipe 33. Tuna Salad

Cooking Time: 0

Servings: 4

The List of Ingredients:

1. 2 tbsp. low-fat sour cream
2. ¼ cup raisins
3. ¼ tsp. Mrs. Dash
4. 1 ½ tsp. curry powder
5. 12 oz. flaked water-packed tuna

6. ½ tsp. cinnamon

7. 1 tsp. Dijon mustard

8. 2 tbsp. chopped celery

9. 2 tbsp. low-fat mayonnaise

10. 2 tbsp. lemon juice

Method:

Step 1   Combine all ingredients in a bowl and refrigerate.

Recipe 34. Glazed Salmon

Cooking Time: 25 minutes

Servings: 4

The List of Ingredients:

1. 2 tbsp. lemon juice
2. ¼ cup maple syrup
3. 1 tsp. red pepper flakes
4. 4 salmon fillets
5. Salt and pepper to taste

6. 1 ½ tsp. Dijon mustard

7. 1 cup chopped cilantro

8. 2 minced garlic cloves

Method:

Step 1   Combine the cilantro, garlic, syrup, red pepper flakes and lemon juice in a small pan.

Step 2   Cook and stir for 5 minutes.

Step 3   Let the mixture cool a bit.

Step 4   Line up the salmon fillets in a baking dish

Step 5   Cover with the marinade and refrigerate for 1 hour.

Step 6   Heat the oven to 375 degrees.

Step 7   Discard most of the marinade and brush the fillets with the mustard and season with salt and pepper

Step 8   Drizzle a few drops of the marinade over the fish.

Step 9   Bake for 20 minutes, or until the salmon is flaky.

Recipe 35. Tuna Patties

Cooking Time: 10 minutes

Servings: 6

The List of Ingredients:

1. 2 tsp. lemon juice
2. 1 cup Panko breadcrumbs or gluten-free breadcrumbs
3. 3 tbsp. canola oil
4. ½ tsp. Dijon mustard

5. 4 tbsp. chopped celery stalk

6. 1 tsp. fat-free mayonnaise

7. ½ tsp. Old Bay Seasoning

8. 2 tbsp. chopped onion

9. Salt and pepper to taste

10. 20 oz. drained canned tuna in water

11. 2 tbsp. grated parmesan cheese

12. 2 beaten eggs

Method:

Step 1   Combine the eggs, mayonnaise, lemon juice, cheese and Panko in a bowl.

Step 2   Gently stir in the tuna, onion, chopped celery and Dijon mustard.

Step 3   Season with salt, pepper and Old Bay Seasoning.

Step 4   Heat the canola oil in a skillet.

Step 5   Create 6 tuna patties and fry for 5 minutes on each side.

Side Dishes

Recipe 36. Cucumber Salad

Cooking Time: 0

Servings: 4

The List of Ingredients:

1. ¼ cup Stevia sweetener
2. 2 tbsp. salt
3. 3 thinly sliced cucumbers
4. 1 tbsp. dill
5. ½ cup cider vinegar

6. 1 cup diced fresh tomatoes

7. 1 sliced red onion

8. 4 tbsp. salt

Method:

Step 1   Place the cucumber slices in a bowl and sprinkle with salt.

Step 2   Refrigerate for 2 hours and rinse the cucumbers and squeeze out all the liquid

Step 3   Combine the sliced cucumber, diced tomatoes and onion and toss.

Step 4   In another bowl, stir together the vinegar, sweetener and ¼ cup of water.

Step 5   Pour the mixture over the cucumbers and stir in the dill.

Step 6   Refrigerate for 2 hours.

Adjust the salt, if needed.

Recipe 37. Mashed Potatoes

Cooking Time: 15 minutes

Servings: 4

The List of Ingredients:

1. 1 tsp. minced garlic
2. Enough chicken broth to cover potatoes
3. 4 cups cubed potatoes
4. Salt and pepper to taste

Method:

Step 1   Heat the chicken broth in a pan.

Step 2   Add the potatoes and minced garlic and cook until the potatoes are soft which should take about 15 minutes.

Step 3   Place the potatoes in a bowl and mash. Add a tbsp. or 2 more chicken broth, if needed.

Step 4   Season with salt and pepper.

Recipe 38. Barley and Beans

Cooking Time: 1 hour 3 minutes

Servings: 6

The List of Ingredients:

1. 1 diced onion
2. ½ cup white wine
3. 2 ½ cup low-sodium chicken broth
4. 1 tsp. olive oil
5. ½ cup uncooked barley

6. 2 cups sliced mushrooms

7. ½ tsp. red pepper flakes

8. ½ cup chopped water chestnuts

9. 1 ½ cup cannellini beans

10. 2 tbsp. minced garlic

Method:

Step 1   Heat the chicken broth and win in a pan and add the barley for 50 minutes.

Step 2   When the barley is almost done, heat the olive oil in a skillet and sauté and onion and mushrooms for 8 minutes.

Step 3   Add the mushroom/onion mixture to the cooked barley and combine.

Step 4   Stir in the water chestnuts, cannellini beans and red pepper flakes and cook for 5 minutes.

Recipe 39. Spicy Lentils

Cooking Time: 35 minutes

Servings: 6

The List of Ingredients:

1. 1 diced onion
2. 1 tbsp. curry powder
3. 1 tbsp. and 1 tsp. olive oil
4. 1 ½ cup fire-roasted chopped tomatoes
5. 1 tsp. Stevia sweetener

6. 1 tsp. cardamom

7. 2 tsp. grated ginger

8. 1 tbsp. garam masala

9. 2 minced garlic cloves

10. 1 tsp. cumin

11. 1 tsp. powder

12. 2 tbsp. red curry paste

13. 2 cups red lentils

14. 1 tsp. onion powder

15. ½ tsp. coriander

Method:

Step 1	Rinse the lentils and place in a pan of water.
Step 2	Cook for 10 minutes or until the lentils are done. Drain and set aside.
Step 3	Combine all spices in a bowl.
Step 4	Heat 1 tbsp. oil and sauté the onion for 15 minutes, until nice and caramelized.
Step 5	Add the garlic and ginger and cook for another 3 minutes.
Step 6	Using another skillet, heat 1 tsp. of olive oil and fry the spices for 2 minutes.
Step 7	Stir the spices into the onions

Step 8   Add the fire-roasted tomatoes and cooked lentils and combine well.

Step 9   Simmer for 5 minutes.

Step 10   Serve with rice.

Recipe 40. Gorgonzola and Pear Salad

Cooking Time: 5 minutes

Servings: 4

The List of Ingredients:

1. 2 tbsp. Stevia sweetener or honey

2. 4 tbsp. Stevia sweetener or honey

3. Salt and pepper to taste

4. 1/3 cup walnut oil

5. 1/3 cup walnut halves

6. ¼ cup crumbled gorgonzola cheese

7. 2 chopped pears

8. 1 small sliced sweet onion

9. 1 bag mixed greens

10. 4 tbsp. cider vinegar

11. 2 tbsp. minced garlic

12. 1 sliced avocado

13. 1 tbsp. Dijon mustard

Method:

Step 1   Combine the walnut halves with 4 tbsp. of sweetener or honey in a skillet and stir for 5 minutes.

Step 2   Place the walnuts on a sheet of waxed paper and let cool.

Step 3   In a bowl, stir together the walnut oil, cider vinegar, 2 tbsp. sweetener or honey, mustard, salt and pepper.

Step 4   Place the mixed greens, pears, gorgonzola cheese, avocado and sweet onion on a platter or in a large bowl.

Step 5   Stir in the dressing and walnuts.

Recipe 41. Orzo and Mushrooms

Cooking Time: 27 minutes

Servings: 6

The List of Ingredients:

1. 2 cups uncooked orzo pasta
2. 2 cups white wine
3. 2 minced garlic cloves
4. Salt and pepper to taste
5. ½ tsp. thyme

6. 1 cup baby spinach

7. 1 tbsp. olive oil

8. 1/3 cup spiced nuts (see recipe) or use regular chopped pecans

9. 1 lb. sliced mushrooms

10. 2 cups low-sodium chicken broth

11. 2 tbsp. sherry

12. 1 chopped onion

Method:

Step 1   Heat the olive oil in a large skillet or pan.

Step 2   Sauté the onions and mushrooms for 8 minutes.

Step 3   Stir in the garlic and cook for another 2 minutes.

Step 4   Add the broth, wine and sherry and bring the liquid to a boil.

Step 5   Add the orzo, salt, pepper and thyme.

Step 6   Cook for 15 minutes.

Step 7   Stir in the spinach and then cook for another 2 minutes, or until the liquid is absorbed.

Step 8   Stir the nuts into the orzo.

Recipe 35. Creamed Spinach

Cooking Time: 15 minutes

Servings: 4

The List of Ingredients:

1. 1 tsp. olive oil
2. ½ cup whipping cream
3. 4 tbsp. white wine
4. Salt and pepper to taste
5. 1 bag baby spinach

6. 2 tbsp. minced garlic
7. 3 tbsp. grated Romano cheese
8. 1 tbsp. balsamic vinegar
9. 1 small diced onion

Method:

Step 1   Place all ingredients except the spinach, cheese, salt and pepper in a skillet.

Step 2   Stir and let simmer for 12 minutes, until some of the liquid evaporates.

Step 3   Add the spinach and season with salt and pepper.

Step 4   Cook for 3 minutes, until the spinach is wilted.

Step 5   Drizzle with Romano cheese.

Desserts

Recipe 42. Chocolate Cake

Cooking Time: 30 minutes

Servings: 8

The List of Ingredients:

1. 1 package unsweetened chocolate pudding mix
2. ¾ cup nonfat chocolate milk
3. 1 cup sugar-free whipped topping
4. 3 egg whites
5. 1 package sugar-free chocolate cake mix

6. 1 package unsweetened chocolate pudding mix

Method:

Step 1   Preheat the oven to 350 degrees.

Step 2   Coat a 10x15 backing dish with a non-stick spray.

Step 3   Combine the chocolate cake mix and the chocolate pudding mix.

Step 4   Stir in 1 ¾ cup water and the egg whites and use a hand mixer to combine for 5 minutes.

Step 5   Transfer the batter to the backing dish.

Step 6   Bake for 30 minutes.

Step 7   While the cake is baking, used a hand mixer to whisk together the chocolate milk and chocolate pudding mix.

Step 8   Fold in the sugar-free topping and frost the cake with the mixture.

Recipe 43. Fruit Salad

Cooking Time: 0

Servings: 8

The List of Ingredients:

1. 2 sliced apples
2. 2 tsp. lemon juice
3. 1 cup halved red grapes
4. 1 ½ cups sliced strawberries
5. 2 sliced bananas

6. 3 cups pineapple chunks with juices

Method:

Step 1   Place the sliced apples and bananas in a bowl
           and drizzle with lemon juice and pineapple
           juice. Let sit 15 minutes.
Step 2   Discard the juice and stir in the pineapple
           chunks, sliced strawberries and grapes.

Recipe 44. Zucchini Brownies

Cooking Time: 31 minutes

Servings: 14

The List of Ingredients:

1. 1 tsp. vanilla
2. 1 ¼ cup grated zucchini
3. ½ cup white flour
4. ½ cup whole-wheat flour
5. ½ cup Stevia sweetener

6. 1 cup chopped 80% or higher dark chocolate

7. 1 tsp. baking soda

8. 1/3 cup unsweetened cocoa

9. ½ cup Truvia brown sugar substitute

10. ½ tsp. salt

11. ¼ cup unsweetened apple sauce

Method:

Step 1   Preheat the oven to 350 degrees.

Step 2   Cover a baking dish with aluminum foil.

Step 3   Place the shaved chocolate in a microwave and melt for 1 minute.

Step 4   Combine both flours, cocoa and salt in a bowl.

Step 5   Stir the melted chocolate and add the apple sauce, both sweeteners, egg and vanilla. Combine well.

Step 6   Add the flour, then the zucchini, to the chocolate mixture and stir.

Step 7   Transfer the batter to the baking dish.

Step 8   Bake for 30 minutes.

Step 9   Let the brownies cool, then cut into pieces.

Recipe 45. Angel Food Cake

Cooking Time: 1 hour.

Servings: 10

The List of Ingredients:

1. 2 tsp. cream of tartar
2. 16 egg whites (freeze the yolks)
3. 1 ¼ cups coconut flour
4. 1 tsp. almond extract

5. Sliced strawberries and sugar-free whipped cream for topping
6. ¼ tsp. salt
7. 1 tsp. vanilla extract
8. 1 ¾ cup date palm sugar or Splenda sweetener

Method:

Step 1   Whip the egg whites with a hand mixer until they are stiff.

Step 2   Stir in the vanilla and almond extract and the cream of tartar.

Step 3   Combine the coconut flour, date palm sugar and salt.

Step 4   Stir the egg whites into the flour.

Step 5   Transfer the batter to a tube pan.

Step 6   Bake at 325 for 1 hour.

Step 7   Let the cake cool.

Step 8   Top with strawberries and sugar-free whipped cream.

Recipe 46. Healthy Oatmeal Cookies

Cooking Time: 20 minutes

Servings: 15

The List of Ingredients:

1. ¼ cup sugar or Stevia sugar substitute
2. 1 cup rolled oats
3. ½ cup white flour
4. ½ tsp. cinnamon
5. ½ tsp. salt

6. ¼ cup Truvia brown sugar substitute

7. ½ cup chopped nuts

8. 2 mashed bananas

9. 1 tsp. baking powder

10. ½ cup whole wheat flower

11. 2 tbsp. water

12. 1/8 tsp. ground cloves

Method:

Step 1   Preheat the oven to 350 degrees.

Step 2   Coat a baking sheet with non-stick spray

Step 3   Combine both sugars and the mashed bananas. Add 2 tbsp. water and stir thoroughly.

Step 4   Stir the remaining ingredients into the banana mixture.

Step 5   Use a tablespoon to drop the dough onto the baking sheet.

Step 6   Bake for 12 minutes.

Printed in the USA
CPSIA information can be obtained
at www.ICGtesting.com
LVHW021459171023
761364LV00005B/494